Helping your pupils
to ask questions

Sally Godinho and Jeni Wilson

Routledge
Taylor & Francis Group

LONDON AND NEW YORK

First published by Curriculum Corporation 2004
PO Box 177
Carlton South Vic 3053
Australia

Reprinted 2006

This edition published 2008 by Routledge
2 Park Square, Milton Park, Abingdon, Oxon, OX14 4RN, United Kingdom

Simultaneously published in the USA and Canada
by Routledge
270 Madison Ave, New York, NY 10016

Routledge is an imprint of the Taylor & Francis Group, an informa business

© 2008 Sally Godinho and Jeni Wilson

Typeset in Stone Serif by FiSH Books, Enfield, Middx.
Printed and bound in Great Britain by TJ International Ltd, Padstow, Cornwall

Dedication
To Ethan and Madison – may they forever ask wonderful questions.

Acknowledgements
Many of the examples in this book were inspired or trialled by practising classroom
teachers. Others have been developed or published with our dear friends and
colleagues. We thank them for their generosity and acknowledge the contributions of
Colleen Abbott, Karen Biggeleau, Dee Clements, Robyn English, Kath Murdoch, Susan
Wilks, Teresa Stone and Lesley Wing Jan. Thanks to the teachers of Ballan P.S.

British Library Cataloguing in Publication Data
A catalogue record for this book is available from the British Library

Library of Congress Cataloging in Publication Data

ISBN 10: 0-415-44727-5
ISBN 13: 978-0-415-44727-0

Contents

1 Why ask questions?   1

2 Types of questions   2

3 The role of the teacher   15

4 Establishing a question-friendly classroom   17

5 Strategies and activities for developing effective questioning   27

6 Frequently asked questions (and troubleshooting)   43

7 Tips for the teacher   49

8 Assessment and record keeping   51

9 Proformas for the classroom   53

10 Further reading   65

Why ask questions?

Asking questions is pivotal to learning how to learn and becoming a lifelong learner. In a technology-driven world, where information overload is often an issue, it is essential that people have the skills to critically question what they view, read and hear. The process of deciding what is relevant, what is of interest, what is legitimate, what is authentic and what requires further investigation involves effective questioning. It is effective questioning that supports informed decision-making.

Questions should always be purpose driven. In the classroom context, there are many purposes for questions and these influence the type of questions that are asked. Teachers often ask questions to facilitate and assess learning, but there are many other specific purposes, such as those listed below.

- Excite interest or curiosity
- Direct pupil thinking in a particular way
- Focus attention on a topic
- Control behaviour of the class or individuals
- Encourage pupils to be actively engaged in learning
- Challenge pupils
- Review pupils' learning
- Reinforce learnt material
- Structure or guide the learning of a task
- Obtain feedback on teaching
- Assess pupils
- Encourage reflection on learning

- Gain feedback from pupils about teaching
- Revision of content
- Help pupils clarify their understandings
- Evaluation purposes
- Model questioning and thinking
- Engage pupils in a particular type of thinking (e.g. critical, creative or reflective)
- Help pupils make connections
- Spark further questions
- Motivate pupil inquiries
- Identify gaps in pupils' learning
- Provide opportunities for pupil learning through discussion

Pupil and teaching needs are of prime importance. An effective teacher question is suited to the purpose and takes the cognitive level of the pupils into consideration. When a question engages pupils and motivates them to ask further questions or challenge their ideas, it has the potential to take pupils beyond their current thinking and engage them in higher-order thinking.

Questions help people make sense of the world. For example: How does that work? What would happen if I reversed the procedure? How would the situation change if I considered it from a different perspective? What might be the result if I changed the variables? What message is the writer trying to convey?

Questioning skills empower people as learners. They are pivotal for solving problems, creating solutions and enacting change. Skilful questioning guides decision-making and the processing, critiquing and challenging of information. Importantly, questioning assists pupils to participate actively in their world and in the wider context of a democratic society.

Types of questions

There are many different types of questions – essential, subsidiary, hypothetical, strategic, provocative, rhetorical, irreverent and content-neutral. The purpose of the question will largely determine the type of question asked.

A very broad way of categorising questions is to typecast them as 'open' or 'closed'. If a question is closed, the answer is non-negotiable and is simply recited; whereas an open-ended question invites interpretation, there being no preconceived response. Open-ended and closed questions are sometimes respectively referred to as divergent and convergent questions, lower-order cognitive and higher-order cognitive questions, or sometimes simplistically in pupil language as fat and skinny questions. While there are subtle differences, these terms are often used interchangeably. *The Open-Ended and Closed Questions* activity (page 28) assists pupils to explore the differences.

The 'What, When, How, Who and Why' can fit into a *product, process and opinion* framework for question planning. These five questions provide contextual background and are often used as a starting point for pupils to organise their thoughts when constructing a recount or a report. Teachers often ask fewer process and opinion questions, but these questions can lead to richer discussions and higher-level thinking.

Product, process and opinion questions

Product	*What, when* and *who* questions: key ideas, facts – details such as time sequence and identifying specific people.
Process	*How* questions are concerned with procedures and processes.
Opinion	*Why* questions consider causal relationships and require explanations.

Three broad categories that might assist when planning a sequence of questions for a lesson or unit of work are: cognitive, affective and creative. It is essential to make these explicit to pupils so that they can expand their ways of considering and generating questions, and develop language skills associated with questioning.

Questions that generate different levels of cognition

Bloom's Taxonomy of Cognitive Processes has recently been revised. The taxonomy was originally devised for curriculum development purposes but is readily adaptable for designing questions that target specific levels of thinking. In the table on page 5, the previous classification terms appear in the left-hand column, so the changes can be noted. The most significant change is that the evaluating level (evaluation) is now perceived as the highest order of thinking, whereas creating (synthesis) previously held this rank. This is consistent with the high value currently placed on creativity in schools and the workplace.

Despite Bloom's Taxonomy being around since the 1950s, it has consistently been shown that classroom questioning is like a quiz show, with teachers asking on average 100–150 questions an hour. This leaves little room for pupils to explore their thinking through exploratory talk and self-initiated questions. Not surprisingly, excessive teacher questioning of this nature has been found to cause anxiety and can be counterproductive in terms of pupil learning.

Both higher- and lower-order cognitive questions can lead to effective learning and have an important role in a questioning repertoire. However, while lower-order questions are often the recommended starting point for establishing basic facts and fundamental understandings, it is the higher-order, big, essential questions that provide pupils with opportunities to construct meaning at a deeper level.

Much depends on the classroom culture and the expectations created. In classrooms where discussion is valued, pupils may turn a closed question into a discussion point. Conversely, an open-ended question may not necessarily induce pupils to engage in higher-order thinking, as raised in the section on handling responses (page 23). The Fairytales activity (page 30) is designed to assist pupils to frame questions that target Bloom's different levels of thinking.

Bloom's Taxonomy

Cognitive level		Processes	Verb stems
Original version	Revised version		
Knowledge	Remembering	Recalling factual information	Name, state, define, repeat, list, recall
Comprehension	Understanding	Understanding information	Explain, identify, describe, compare, report, outline, tell, locate, review
Application	Applying	Using previously learnt knowledge, concepts, principles or theories in new situations	Apply, practise, use, demonstrate, illustrate, dramatise, interpret
Analysis	Analysing	Breaking information into parts and showing an understanding between the parts	Analyse, contrast, compare, question, debate, relate, examine, identify
Synthesis	Creating (now highest level)	Generating new ideas, planning and producing	Compose, propose, suggest, plan, design, construct, invent, formulate, create, arrange, prepare
Evaluation	Evaluating	Critiquing, making a judgement on the values or consistency of a process, product or idea	Judge, assess, decide, rate, evaluate, measure, estimate, choose

Self-questioning and self-talk: reflective and metacognitive questions

Questions that elicit reflection and metacognition are very important. Some argue that reflection and metacognition are central to learning. They assist in monitoring and self-regulating learning, particularly in pupil-centred classrooms.

Modelling self-questioning and self-talk is essential in helping pupils to be reflective and metacognitive. The table below provides examples of reflective and metacognitive questions that support pupils to develop as reflective and metacognitive thinkers and questioners. Use the question strips (pages 55–6) to engage pupils in reflection and metacognition.

Reflective and metacognitive questions

Type of question	Description	Examples
REFLECTIVE		
Teacher reflection on teaching practice	Reflective questions engage the learner/ thinker in deliberate, purposeful consideration of the effectiveness of actions and experiences.	What were the strengths of this lesson/unit? What were its weaknesses? What activities were successful for pupil learning? How useful were the assessment tasks?
Teacher questions to elicit pupil reflections		What team skills did your group use? What did you like about the activity/excursion? What could have been done to make the activity more useful?
Pupil reflections		What did I contribute to the group? What aspects of my/our group work need to be improved? What skills have I improved in this unit?
METACOGNITIVE		
Teacher metacognition of teaching practice	Metacognitive questions focus on the learner's awareness, evaluation and regulation of their own thinking. When using metacognition, questions relate to making decisions, choosing appropriate strategies and thinking processes, self-assessing their own thinking, planning action and goal setting.	What resources will I use? How will I determine pupils' prior knowledge? How am I best able to support pupils' learning? What did I learn about the way pupils process information? What goals do I now need to set for my teaching and learning? What would I do differently next time?

Type of question	Description	Examples
Teacher questions to elicit pupil metacognition		Why might we be studying this topic? How might you start this task? What do you need to think about to complete the task? What are your big questions? How has your thinking changed? What sort of thinking would be useful for this task? What goals do you need to set for your learning?
Pupil metacognitive questions		What do I already know about this topic? What do I want to find out? What questions do I have? How will I source the information? How have my ideas changed over this unit? What did I learn? What learning strategy worked best for me? How well did I meet my learning goals?

Questions to encourage pupils to think more deeply

A very effective way to engage pupils in deeper-level thinking is to take a philosophical approach to questioning (see Lipman 1988; Wilks 1995). A Philosophy for Children approach requires special training to develop the skills required to facilitate philosophical discussion.

However, Clinton Golding's generic thought-provoking questions (see the table opposite) provide a useful tool for supporting pupils to take responsibility for thinking more deeply, and generating more considered responses to questions. These questions require pupils to clarify, justify and extend their ideas and opinions. The generic question cards (page 58) provide a great way to familiarise yourself with these prompts, but it is important to ask questions that relate specifically to issues or ideas that pupils raise. The questions below are categorised into three headings; inevitably, there is some crossover.

Questions that ask for depth	Questions that ask for reasoning	Questions that ask for clarification
What other points need to be taken into consideration? What might be the implications or consequences? How can we build on this idea? What questions would you need to ask? Who has another perspective?	Why did you think that? Does that follow? How do you know? What are some possible explanations? Is that a good enough reason? How could we prove this? How is that different from what was said? How do you know?	Why did you say that? Do you agree or disagree? Is that what you meant? What have we found out? What did we do well? What could we improve? What questions would be useful to ask? When would that not happen? Are those ideas consistent? What does that tell us?

Thought-provoking questions

Questions that ask for reasons	Why did you say that?
Questions that ask for evaluation of reasons	What reasons support that idea?
Questions that ask for clarification	Is that what you meant?
Questions that ask for explanations	What are some possible causes?
Questions that ask for evidence	How could we prove this?
Questions that ask for definitions	What does that mean?
Questions that ask for counter examples	When would that not happen?
Questions that ask for alternatives	What would be a different view?
Questions that probe assumptions	How do you know?
Questions that ask for consequences and implications	What would the consequences be?
Questions that ask for connections	Do those two ideas agree?
Questions that ask for distinctions	How is that different from what was said?
Questions that ask for questions	What questions would be useful to ask?
Questions that ask for summary of the content	What have we found out?
Questions that ask for a summary of the process	What did we do well? What could we improve?

(Adapted from Golding 2002)

The questions in this table are not hierarchical in the way that Bloom's Taxonomy lists the cognitive levels from the least to the most challenging. They simply serve as reminders of the sort of probing questions that need to be asked if pupils are to become critical, creative and logical thinkers.

Using a 'cheat sheet' during a small group or class discussion might be of assistance in applying and modelling these generic questions. A useful strategy to encourage pupils to use the questions would be to have them on laminated strips and placed in the centre of the table as a reference point during a small group discussion. (See the questions on pages 55–6.)

Questions that focus on emotional responses

Questions that address our feelings and emotions are associated with the affective domain. They are central to our hearts and souls and are sometimes referred to as essential questions (McKenzie 2000). These questions probe complex matters that elude simple answers. Examples of these questions include:

> What does it mean to have integrity?
> Who do I consider to be somebody with integrity?
> What does it mean to be a good friend?
> Who do I consider to be my good friends?
> How can I be a better friend?

Krathwohl *et al.*'s (1964) Affective Domain Taxonomy is concerned with emotional responses, and was designed to complement Bloom's Taxonomy. While not as widely known to educators as Bloom's Taxonomy, its significance should not be overlooked. Chambers (1994), known for his work in developing literature circles and enhancing the quality of pupil discussion, advocates the importance of starting with questions that address pupils' emotional responses before moving on to more directed questions.

Typical questions would be:

> What did you like the most?
> Was there anything you did not like?
> What was something that puzzled you?
> Was there anything that made a pattern?

These questions connect with the receiving level of Krathwohl *et al.*'s Taxonomy. Responding emotionally generally gets pupils engaged in a discussion. Chambers suggests that by using the 'tell me' approach, where the question is implied rather than explicit, pupils feel more relaxed and less threatened. Applying a more conversational tone allows pupils to gain confidence before the more probing questions that require deeper-level thinking are approached.

A constant stream of questions can appear like an interrogation to pupils and can quickly shut down the talk. This style of questioning is rarely experienced outside the classroom, with the exceptions of a police interview or courtroom scenario.

Krathwohl *et al.*'s Instructional Objectives for the Affective Domain

Cognitive level	Instructional objectives	Useful verbs for framing questions
Receiving	Listening or attending closely	Recall, recognise, observe, select, reply, use, feel, identify, describe
Responding	Showing active interest or enjoyment	Answer, assist, compile, discuss, perform, present, tell, label, practise, report
Valuing	Demonstrating commitment, concern or involvement	Complete, form, join, justify, report, share, select, argue, study, persuade
Organisation	Constructing a value system	Adhere, alter, arrange, combine, compare, define, explain, identify, modify, synthesise, defend, integrate, articulate
Characterisation by a value or value complex	Acting in accordance to an established value system	Discriminate, display, influence, qualify, question, revise, solve, verify, propose, review, judge, resolve, rate, conclude

Some examples of using Krathwohl *et al.*'s Taxonomy to frame implicit questions include:

Describe the impact of bullying on pupils. (Receiving)
Compile a list of the different types of bullying. (Responding)
Propose ways of addressing bullying in school. (Characterisation)

While not direct questions, pupils generally know that a response is expected. Affective questioning aligns with de Bono's Red Hat thinking, which is discussed on page 39.

Questioning for creative thinking

There are eight processes identified with creative thinking. Fluency, flexibility, originality and elaboration align with the cognitive domain (thinking abilities); and curiosity, complexity, risk taking and imagination with the affective domain (feeling abilities). Higher-order thinking skills and creativity go hand-in-hand. The next table provides some suggestions for framing questions that encourage pupils to think creatively.

The importance of divergent thinking should not be underestimated. As previously suggested, it is important to be creative in the way questions are framed and in terms of their content. Be prepared to challenge and surprise pupils so that they have to think 'outside the square'. Creativity does not always occur immediately or spontaneously. Try wearing a ridiculous hat or unusual item of clothing to class and wait for pupils to generate questions. Don't provide the answer to their questions; turn the questions back to the pupils: What reasons might there be for looking like this today?

An alternative model for encouraging divergent thinking includes seven different question types and connects across the affective and cognitive domains. The table on page 13 shows what each type of question means and provides some generic examples.

Processes associated with creative thinking

	Description	Examples
Fluency	Generating many ideas	Brainstorm different ideas about how technology will change teaching and learning. List all the ideas you have for re-using damaged CD-ROMs or DVDs.
Flexibility	Generating varied, different or alternative ideas	What other perspectives are there to consider? What are all the different ways you could travel to school? What other ways could this problem be solved?
Originality	Generating unusual, unique or new ideas	A wild card scenario might be . . . ? What words might you have spoken had you been the first person to step on the moon?
Elaboration	Generating enriched, embellished or expanded ideas	How could you extend this idea to ...? How could I make the cover of *Snow White and the Seven Dwarfs* appeal to teenagers? If you wanted to get younger children interested in this book what would you say?
Risk taking	Experimenting with and exploring ideas	If you took an opposite tack what might the outcomes be? If you had to complete your schooling in a non-English speaking country, what might be some of your experiences? If plastic bags were banned, what would some of the alternatives and consequences be?
Complexity	Improving and explaining ideas	What other layer could we add to ...? How might public transport look 100 years from today? What would happen if we added ...? How could we change the end result?
Curiosity	Pondering and questioning ideas	What if you had wings? How might the government work differently if children were allowed to vote?
Imagination	Visualising and fantasising ideas	Imagine that you were President of the USA for one day. What would you do? Think about what it would be like if there were two shifts of school each day.

(Adapted from Dalton 1985 & Gross *et al.* 2001)

Divergent thinking model

Type of question	Description	Example
Quantity	Quantitative examination, for example, number, size, proportion	How many ...? What examples can you give? What proportion should be given to ...?
Change	Creative thinking. Elements may be substituted	What if you? What would happen if one element was changed?
Prediction	Hypotheses, predicting possible future actions, consequences, outcomes	What might happen if ...? What could be a consequence? What would your hypothesis be? What do you think you might see/find?
Point of view	Give opinion and justify	What different points of view are you aware of? What would be another way of seeing this? What's your opinion? Could you extend your idea by considering another perspective?
Personal involvement	Personal point of view	If you could ... If you were ... What's your point of view?
Comparative association	Compare and contrast	If you were to compare ... what might you find? What are the differences and similarities between these ...?
Valuing	Feelings	What is your opinion? What is important to you? How do you feel?

(Adapted from Dalton 1985)

SCAMPER (Substitute, Combine, Adapt, Modify, Magnify or Minimise, Put to use, Eliminate and Rearrange) is a useful creative questioning strategy (see page 39). Like all strategies, it should not be overused. It should be one of several questioning strategies in the questioning toolbox to encourage creative thinking. For further reading about creative questioning approaches refer to Dalton (1985) and see the Wiederhold Q-Matrix activity on page 29.

Teacher questions to guide planning

Teachers should think about the types of questions they would ask as part of the planning process. The following questions may be useful to help reflect on the strategies, structures and support given to developing effective questions in the classroom.

	Usually	Some-times	Never
Do I model a variety of questions and questioning strategies?			
Do I think about the purpose of the question?			
Do I include questions when planning?			
Do I make time for pupils to ask questions and find out the answers for themselves?			
Have I organised opportunities for pupils to adopt different questioning roles?			
Do I use pupil prior knowledge to help further their ideas?			
Do I encourage pupils to discuss their thinking?			
Do I show that I am interested in different types of questions?			
Do I use self-assessment to elicit self-questioning?			
Do I use probing questions rather than just accept the first answer to questions?			
Do I explain why I asked a particular question?			
Do I verbalise questions about my own actions?			
Do I encourage pupils to listen to each other and question each other?			
Do I encourage pupils to listen to a range of possible answers?			
Have I established an environment where pupils feel free to ask questions and take risks?			
Do I allow wait time for pupils to answer questions?			
Do I listen to pupil ideas and build on their responses?			

The role of the teacher

Effective teacher questioning challenges pupils intellectually and sometimes emotionally. Questions seek to focus discussion and thinking, and are appropriate for the cognitive range of learners in the classroom. Effective teacher questioning is mindful of the purpose and the context. Questions are predominantly open-ended, thought provoking and non-judgemental.

To utilise effective questioning:

■ Plan some questions in advance. Build up to the more challenging questions so that pupils have time to gain confidence.

■ Focus on a few carefully constructed open-ended questions, rather than a quick succession of closed questions typical of a quiz show approach (unless that is the purpose).

■ Frame questions as clearly and concisely as possible to avoid ambiguity.

■ Ask one question at a time. A string of questions is very confusing for pupils.

■ Consider the need for think time. Avoid the trap of answering your own question because pupils are seemingly slow to respond.

■ Vary the strategies used so that questioning does not become predictable. Plan a few surprises. For example, make a provocative statement and wait for a response, rather than asking a direct question.

■ Ensure every pupil has the opportunity to respond to some questions by catering for the range of learners in the classroom.

Teachers can encourage effective pupil questions by what they say, the way they provide feedback to pupil responses, use silence, accept and clarify pupil questions, and by their responsiveness. Points to consider for helping pupils to ask effective questions include:

- building a shared language for questioning
- introducing different questioning strategies (see pages 27–41) and discussing these with pupils
- developing pupil awareness of different types of questions and what type of thinking they require (see pages 3–14)
- making space for pupil questions and celebrating them.

For example:

Teacher	What questions does this article raise for you?
Pupil	If there were animals on Earth before humans, how come humans developed authority?
Teacher	That was a really interesting question that Sam asked. Would anyone like to respond?

This book encourages teachers to think about how questioning is critical both for their own learning and their pupils' learning. The proformas on pages 56 and 58 encourage pupils to focus on quality questions and design some of their own.

Establishing a question-friendly classroom

Who asks the questions in a classroom? In some classrooms there is an expectation that the teacher will be the question-asker and pupils the question-answerers. The classroom culture needs to encourage pupils to be both the question-askers and question-answerers.

In classrooms where pupil-centred learning occurs, such as an inquiry approach to teaching and learning, an excellent context for pupils to ask questions exists. For example, at the tuning in stage, questions that drive the inquiry are: What do I already know? What do I need to find out? What questions do I have about this topic? What aspects of this topic really interest me? How will I find the information? In classrooms where the inquiry approach is embedded in practice, pupil questions are usually on display. Pupils are encouraged to revisit these questions and to seek answers to them. An example of pupil questions for different stages of the inquiry process is provided on page 45.

Similarly, in classrooms that embrace Philosophy for Children, pupils' questions are valued. Pupils learn which questions best drive the discussion of issues and big ideas. The inquiry approach and Philosophy for Children are dependent upon establishing a classroom culture in which teachers and pupils understand their responsibilities.

Questions in a philosophical inquiry address a wide range of issues that impact on our lives. Pupils learn that some issues can be resolved, some can only be temporarily resolved and some have no resolution. Examples of philosophical questions that could be used to generate a discussion include:

- Do all creatures have a mind? What has a mind?
- Does saying sorry mean that inappropriate behaviour should be forgiven?
- Is it ever acceptable to break a rule? Is so, when do you think it is acceptable?

- Should all people be treated equally? Can you think of times when people should not all be treated equally?
- What counts as being intelligent?

Questioning with the whole class, small groups and individual pupils

Approaches to questioning may vary slightly in accordance with the teaching and learning context – whole class, small group or individual pupil. However, while most of the principles for effective questioning are relevant for all contexts, there are a few differences in approach.

Whole class

Ensuring all pupils stay engaged can be challenging. In order to manage the whole class dynamic, more control of the questioning process is essential. A few points to remember include:

- Be inclusive. It's easy to focus on the pupils who give the more considered, interesting responses.
- Redirect questions so that several pupils can respond.
- Summarise responses (if several responses have been given) to keep the class focused.
- Make explicit your expectations about appropriate ways to respond. For example, calling out and interrupting a pupil's talk-turn is unacceptable.

Small group

Small group learning offers greater opportunities for pupils to build their question-asking and question-answering skills. In this context, it is easier to distribute questions more evenly and to take the time to probe pupils' responses, assisting them to clarify tentative ideas through exploratory talk. It is also easier for the teacher to step back from a more controlling role, thereby encouraging pupils to respond to one another.

Pupils also need opportunities to lead their own small group learning in discussions and group conferences. This puts the onus squarely on the pupils to ask the questions, rather than relying on the teacher. When pupils question each other about their learning it has the potential to generate higher-level thinking.

Individual pupil

One-to-one scenarios in a conference situation provide excellent opportunities for pupils to reflect on their learning; and for teachers to monitor pupil learning and elicit what assistance is needed. Questions need to be carefully framed so that the pupil doesn't feel a sense of interrogation. In this context, question-asking and question-answering should be viewed as joint responsibilities shared between teacher and pupil. Some key responsibilities for both teachers and pupils that apply across teaching and learning contexts are listed in the following tables.

Pupil responsibilities

Take initiative as a question-asker	Don't wait for someone else to take the initiative or think that it is the teacher's role to ask the questions.
Be a risk taker	Sometimes you may be unsure how to frame your question. Go ahead and ask, as verbalising may help clarify what you want to know. Be prepared to ask questions that challenge or contest somebody else's point of view.
Explore tentative and emergent ideas	Ask questions that help you clarify and extend your ideas or explore alternative possibilities: ■ Am I right in thinking that ...? ■ Is it possible that ...? ■ What might ...? ■ What if ...? ■ How could ...?
Self-monitor and regulate your learning	Ask questions that help you make decisions about your learning, self-assess your progress and set future goals. ■ What do I do well? ■ What can I improve? ■ What goals will I set myself?

Teacher responsibilities

Create an atmosphere of trust	Pupils need to have your support and that of their peers when they ask and respond to questions.
Model different types of questioning	Pupils need to see you modelling questions in the three broad domains: cognitive (thinking), affective (feeling) and creative.
Adopt different questioning roles	Pupils need to adopt different roles when asking questions. **Facilitator:** assist with the development of ideas <ul><li>What makes you say that?</li><li>What is another way of looking at it?</li><li>Who has a different view?</li></ul> **Provoker:** challenge opinions or play devil's advocate <ul><li>What evidence do you have?</li><li>How do you know that?</li></ul> **Monitor:** draw attention to the reasoning processes <ul><li>Is this a logical conclusion?</li><li>What would be the consequences?</li></ul> **Mediator:** assist in resolving differences <ul><li>Can we reach some consensus?</li><li>What do we agree upon?</li></ul>
Familiarise pupils with a range of questioning and thinking strategies	Pupils need encouragement to apply strategies such as: Six Thinking Hats (page 38), Bloom's Taxonomies (page 5), the Q-Matrix (page 29), Thought-Provoking Questions (page 8).
Create space for pupil questions	Make time for pupil questions.

Encouraging responses and questions

It is important to make explicit your expectations about pupils being active question-askers. Pupils may not have been encouraged to take this role previously. One approach is to jointly construct a chart identifying behaviours associated with a classroom culture that values questioning. This can be a powerful way of collaboratively building expectations about questioning.

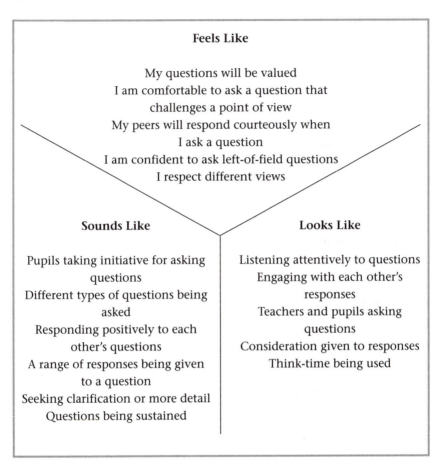

Feels Like

My questions will be valued
I am comfortable to ask a question that
challenges a point of view
My peers will respond courteously when
I ask a question
I am confident to ask left-of-field questions
I respect different views

Sounds Like

Pupils taking initiative for asking
questions
Different types of questions being
asked
Responding positively to each
other's questions
A range of responses being given
to a question
Seeking clarification or more detail
Questions being sustained

Looks Like

Listening attentively to questions
Engaging with each other's
responses
Teachers and pupils asking
questions
Consideration given to responses
Think-time being used

Creating a T chart is another way of collaboratively constructing understandings about what it means to be a class that values asking questions as a means of building knowledge and clarifying meaning. In response to the prompts: 'A question-friendly classroom is/is not ...', pupils write statements about their beliefs and values.

A questioning-friendly classroom is a place where:	A questioning-friendly classroom is not a place where:
different responses to a question are encouraged	pupil responses to questions are put down
pupils build on each other's responses	teachers are seen as the question-askers and pupils as the question-answerers
pupils are prepared to challenge or contest a response	pupils recite a response to a question rather than discuss it
pupils take risks and offer divergent ideas and opinions	pupils are concerned with expressing their viewpoint rather than responding to what someone else has said
pupils generate questions for discussions	

Alternatively, a mission statement could be prepared that defines a question-friendly classroom. There are many other creative ways of constructing shared expectations, such as:

- role-play scenarios
- posters
- cartoon strips
- raps with musical accompaniment.

Pupils can also generate their own ideas to demonstrate what they know about a question-friendly classroom.

The expectation that pupils will initiate questions must be demonstrated by creating space for pupil questions within lesson planning. Some methods for encouraging pupils to be question-askers follow.

- When pupils ask questions, respond positively and attentively. Teachers often give scant time to pupil questions because they may divert the focus of the lesson. Positive acknowledgement and responding or turning the question back to the class or group demonstrates that pupil questions are valued.

- Create spaces by remembering to ask: What questions were raised for you by doing this activity? What questions does this text raise? What questions do you have about today's class plan?

- Begin a new topic by asking what questions pupils have. These can be listed, displayed and referred to as the topic develops.

- Compile a list of questions pupils have before beginning a topic discussion. The questions can then be sorted into questions with answers that can be readily located, and those related to issues or ideas that require exploration through discussion.

- Model questions that seek to clarify thinking. For example: 'I wasn't sure what the author meant by saying that. What do you think the writer is trying to say here?' Be prepared to express uncertainty and openly question an authoritative text.

- Ask pupils to use Post-it notes to write down questions that come to mind as they read. These can then be brought to class to generate discussion.

- Introduce some of the games and strategies (page 27) that build pupils' skills in constructing questions.

Handling responses to questions

The way teachers encourage and receive pupil responses to questions transmits very explicit messages about their expectations of pupil learning and the classroom culture. Pupils are often concerned about how their responses to questions might be perceived by their teacher and/or their peers. Therefore, establishing trust is essential so pupils will be prepared to take risks and share ideas that are different or divergent, rather than conformist and reflective of groupthink.

Sometimes teacher responses suggest to pupils that a game of 'guess what is inside my head' is being played. In some instances of directed teaching this may be quite appropriate. However, if the purpose of questioning is discussion, directing pupils to predetermined answers defeats the opportunity of open-ended questions. Furthermore, when pupils think that a particular answer is required (or valued) it might discourage them from responding to questions or from responding honestly. In the following example, note the way in which the teacher's responses to pupil ideas reduce an open-ended question to a closed question with a predetermined answer.

Teacher	What does war cost?
Pupil	It costs love.
Teacher	Yes, good.
Pupil	It costs lives.
Teacher	Costs lives, certainly.
Pupil	It costs freedom.
Teacher	Yes, we had it here. Great point, but you haven't got it.
Pupil	Identity.
Teacher	Good but it wasn't what I was thinking of. I'll give you a clue. What didn't he have?
Pupil	Love.
Teacher	Partly.
Pupil	Childhood and love.
Teacher	Childhood. That's the one I like.

Despite the insightfulness of the pupil responses, the teacher's eagerness to elicit the 'right' answer to the question means probes, such as 'What do you mean by saying it costs freedom?', are not used and opportunities to expand the pupils' thinking and develop discussion are overlooked. In this excerpt, the QRQ sequence (teacher question, pupil response, teacher question) strategy might have been much more productive in terms of developing discussion than the IRE sequence (initiation of question by teacher, response by pupil, evaluation of pupil response by teacher). Some strategies that may assist in handling pupil responses to questions are presented in the table opposite.

It is also important for pupils to learn about responding to each other appropriately, particularly when contesting a peer's response to a question. Reliance on teacher modelling of appropriate ways to challenge an idea or opinion may not always be sufficient. Some explicit teaching of the skills through an activity can assist pupils to acquire the language required for framing such responses, and prevent disputational talk. This talk form is offensive and may cause pupils to withdraw from a discussion.

Providing pupils with some assistance in rehearsing responses to a contested idea is a useful strategy. For example:

Have you considered the point of view of ...?
What about considering this point of view ...?
I agree with what you say, but I also think ...
Another way of looking at the situation is ...
Yes, but what would you think if ...?
That's one way, but another possibility is ...

Handling pupil responses

Strategy	Description	Application
Demonstrate active listening	Show pupils you are interested in their response. Initial responses may be fragmented or disjointed as pupils grapple to clarify their ideas.	Use non-verbal signals such as facial expressions, a nod, eye contact, sitting forward.
Sustain the question	Use follow-up probes that encourage the clarification, extension or elaboration of a response. Encourage a range of responses to the one question.	Does anyone have a different opinion? Could you tell us a little more about that idea? Can you provide some evidence to support your point of view?
Allow wait time	Learn to be comfortable with the silences, so that wait time is extended. Tell pupils why you are waiting.	Use affirmative non-verbal signals (such as a nod) that show engagement and provide encouragement.
Minimise feedback	Affirm pupil responses, but avoid excessive praise, which may silence alternative responses.	That's an interesting view. Yes, that's one way. Can anyone add to that? Thank you for that idea.
Vacate the floor	Redirect pupil responses or comments. Breaking the IRE sequence makes pupils aware that talk doesn't always have to be directed through the teacher. This encourages pupil dialogue.	Would any one like to respond to that idea? What can you add to that response? How consistent is this response with your thinking?

Encourage pupils to develop their own lead-ins to challenging a response. Their examples and the ones listed above could be recorded on a chart or strips and used by pupils during small group discussions.

Ensuring that pupils feel comfortable about challenging a response to a question should not be underestimated. Without the necessary skills, pupils may be reluctant to contribute alternative perspectives and ideas, resulting in conformity or a groupthink approach to discussion. If your aim is for pupils to explore ideas through open-ended, higher-order questions, they must learn to value a diversity of opinions and ideas.

The *All Views Considered* activity (page 37) is designed to help pupils accept and respect that other people have a right to their views and to challenge and question their ideas respectfully.

Strategies and activities for developing effective questioning

The following activities and strategies have many possible adaptations and can be used with different age groups. Most of them involve pupils asking questions and using higher-order thinking. They are best used within a meaningful context, such as the current classroom topic, rather than as an isolated activity. However, they may be used to demonstrate the importance of effective questioning. Make the associated purpose of the activity or strategy explicit and always follow up with some focused discussion on the implications and/or applications for pupils' learning.

The five whys

Purpose: Develop the skill of using probes to extend a response or acquire more in-depth information.

This is a paired activity where one person takes the role of a questioner and the other answers the questions. After each response the questioner uses the response to create a new 'why' question. Each person needs to listen carefully to the other. The pair aims to ask five questions that get a new, usually more in-depth answer.

For example:

Question: Why do we have a school canteen?
Response: Because people want to buy lunch.
Question: Why do people want to buy lunch?
Response: Because they prefer bought lunches than home lunches.
Question: Why do people prefer lunches from the canteen?

NB: The 'five' is a random number, therefore it is more important that pupils listen and think carefully about their questions and responses than necessarily reaching the fifth question. It is interesting to hear where each pair ends up – the final question and response.

Topic question dice

Purpose: Evaluate pupil learning in an informal engaging way that provides an element of fun.

Write questions related to the current topic on masking tape and stick onto a large die. Pupils sit in a circle and one person at a time rolls the die and responds to the question.

Example questions:

What is one way to group living things?
What can be done to control the waste of materials?
What can people do to stay healthy?
What community services does the community have to offer?

Open-ended and closed questions

Purpose: Help pupils differentiate between closed questions and open-ended questions.

Example closed question: What was the name of the artist?
Example open question: What message do you think the artist was trying to convey?

Write one topic word on a sticky label for each class member. For example, food types, animals or fiction titles. Stick one label on each pupil's back. Advise them that to guess what is written on their label. Pupils may only ask questions that elicit a yes or no response. Explain that these questions are termed 'closed questions' as they usually relate to factual information and do not require pupils to engage in deeper-level thinking. Pupils may only ask one question per person.

Alternatively, sit three pupils in a circle. Each pupil wears a hat with a sticky label attached, which is not visible to them. The pupils ask the class closed questions to determine what is on their label.

Discuss the benefits and disadvantages of questioning in this way. Discuss any strategies that pupils may have developed to find the answer.

Use postcards to demonstrate the way an open-ended question is constructed. As a class, jointly construct five open-ended questions relating to the picture on the postcard. In small groups, pupils practise writing open-ended questions for their postcards. Questions and cards are exchanged and each group uses their postcard and set of postcards for a small group discussion.

Weiderhold's Q-matrix

Purpose: Support the development of questions that target different thinking levels, ranging from the simplest levels (recall) to complex levels that require pupils to synthesise and evaluate.

	Event	Situation	Choice	Person	Reason	Means
Present	What is?	Where/ when is?	Which is?	Who is?	Why is?	How is?
Past	What did?	Where/ when did?	Which did?	Who did?	Why did?	How did?
Possibility	What can?	Where/ when can?	Which can?	Who can?	Why can?	How can?
Probability	What would?	Where/ when would?	Which would?	Who would?	Why would?	How would?
Prediction	What will?	Where/ when will?	Which will?	Who will?	Why will?	How will?
Imagination	What might?	Where/ when might?	Which might?	Who might?	Why might?	How might?

The Q-matrix can be used in many ways. Here are some ideas:

1. Put all the key words onto flashcards. Make two different coloured sets: one with what, where, which, who, why and how; and another set with is, did, can, would, will and might. Pupils select a card from each set and brainstorm all the questions they can think of with those words in it. For example: How might we complete this task? How might the day be re-organised to include more games?
2. Put a set of words from the previous idea onto the sides of two large dice. Throw the dice and use the results to list questions.
3. Give pupils one strip of the matrix, such as the 'Who' questions to help them get started in writing activities.
4. Use particular questions to encourage higher-order thinking. The questions in the bottom right nine cells are the most complex.

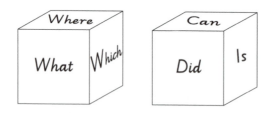

Fairytales

Purpose: Familiarise pupils with the different levels of thinking that can be required by a question.

Introduce pupils to the following set of questions designed around Bloom's Taxonomy for the story *Little Red Riding Hood*. Groups of pupils each take a different fairytale or story and design a set of questions matched to Bloom's levels of thinking.

Remembering	Where did Little Red Riding Hood's grandmother live?
Understanding	What was the purpose of Little Red Riding Hood's visit to her grandmother?

Applying	If your grandmother was sick and you went to visit her, what would you take her?
Analysing	Why do you think Little Red Riding Hood did not recognise that the wolf had disguised himself as her grandmother?
Evaluating	Do you think Little Red Riding Hood's mother behaved responsibly sending her to visit grandma on her own?
Creating	How might the story have been different if Little Red Riding Hood had taken her mobile phone?

Examples of pupil questions after reading *The Tortoise and the Hare*:

- Why was the hare so stupid when he could have won the race easily?
- Why did the hare wake up so late?
- How could a tortoise win a race?
- Why did the tortoise think he'd win?
- What if the hare hadn't had a nap?
- What if people were as slow as the tortoise?

Creative questioning

Purpose: Encourage pupils to develop questions that encourage creative thinking and emotive responses.

Use multiple sets of cards with question types written on them as follows.

Prediction/ imagination	What if...? What would happen if...? What could happen if...?
Quantity questions	List all the things... How many ways...?
Compare and contrast questions	How is it the same? How is it different?

Emotion and motivation	Make 'em laugh; make 'em mad; make 'em sad. (Discuss a controversial issue. Be provocative.)
Point of view	How would an ant feel about an elephant?

Collect a set of stimulus pictures or a selected group of photocopied articles from the newspaper and organise the pupils into small groups. Provide groups with a stimulus picture or an article, and a set of question type cards. Each group prepares at least one question to match the question type. Pupils can then answer each others' questions.

Talk and question counters

Purpose: Draw attention to the paucity of pupil questions and encourage pupils to use them as a means of initiating discussion.

In a small group discussion distribute five yellow counters (responses) and five blue counters (questions) to each participant. Explain that each time a participant responds to a question or makes a comment, a yellow counter must be returned to a centrally placed tub; likewise a blue counter when a question is asked.

Once all counters are used up, participants must allow other pupils the same opportunity to use all their counters. Although the counters can make discussions disjointed, the importance of listening and posing useful questions is exposed.

Lucky dip questions

Purpose: Encourage pupils to be effective and reflective question-askers.

Use questions from the Q-matrix activity (page 29), question strips (pages 55–6) or questions specific to your own topic, in a lucky dip box (or envelope) and have pupils pick one out to answer. This makes a great tuning in or reflection activity.

What's in the box?

Purpose: Develop strategic questioning skills by applying the process of elimination.

Place an object in a box and wrap it as a present. Tell pupils they cannot guess what's in it until they are absolutely sure. They must ask questions about the object and they will be told if they are right or not. If they guess the answer incorrectly the game is over.

Example question	Y/N
Is it alive?	No
Was it ever alive?	No
Is it round?	Yes
Is it bigger than a hand?	No
Is it soft?	No
Is it solid?	No
Is it white?	Yes
Is it breakable?	Yes
Is it an egg?	Yes

Who/what am I?

Purpose: Make pupils aware of how the wording of a question can limit responses to one-word answers, and encourage pupils to be strategic questioners by applying the process of elimination.

In this game pupils are secretly given a name of a place, animal, etc., and others have to ask them questions to guess who or what they are. They can only answer yes or no.

Celebrity heads

Purpose: Encourage pupils to be strategic questioners.

This is similar to *Who am I?* (page 33) except pupils are given a word to place on their heads that they have not seen. Select three or four pupils to sit at the front of the class facing the others. To guess the word they ask questions of the audience. If they are correct they get another chance to ask another question. If they are incorrect they have to wait for another turn. The game ends when one person guesses the word on their head. A clue might be given at the beginning to narrow the guessing field, for example, they are all mammals.

Stop, think and question

Purpose: Encourage pupils to use questions as springboards to further their understanding of a topic.

This strategy can be used at any time and during any subject. Ask pupils to stop, think and jot down any question that comes into their head. These questions can be used for many purposes, for example, further reflective journal writing, self-assessment, group discussions or a class brainstorm list.

- Is water like wood? Is there always the same amount of water in the world?
- How did we get seeds before there were any trees?
- Why were people made? They just destroy the Earth. Were they made for a purpose?

Take a stand

Purpose: Develop the skills of question-asking and question-answering, and of evaluating responses to questions.

The class is divided into three groups. One group must take a position on a problem and another group takes the opposite position. The third group develops a list of questions for both groups. After hearing the responses from both groups, the third group must make a considered decision about how the problem might be solved.

Wear my shoes or see through my specs

Purpose: Ask questions that take into account other perspectives and points of view.

Pupils try to imagine being in someone else's shoes. For example: A war is about to break out in your city. What questions might be asked by the local citizens, the military, the families of those in the military services, etc?

Alternatively, provide a range of old glasses and have pupils put them on. These act as props. Pupils try to see the issue being discussed though different perspectives.

The answer is ?

Purpose: Encourage pupils to ask creative and divergent questions.

Give pupils a word or a number and tell them that is the answer. Ask them to come up with as many questions as they can. This is lots of fun and can be adapted in many ways. For example, at the end of a unit give different groups different 'answers' related to the topic in secret envelopes. Their task is to come up with one brilliant question so that when they read it to the class everyone will know their answer.

If you were the teacher

Purpose: Ask questions that take into account other perspectives or points of view.

Pupils pretend to be the teacher and try to understand their actions. Some possible questions include:

- If you were the teacher what would you do? What would you do differently?
- How would you assist someone who needed help?
- Why do you think I did this activity?
- What was the purpose of this task?
- What should I do next to help everybody learn?

Alternatively, ask pupils to lead a discussion. What questions would they ask of their pupils? This can be very interesting and sometimes confrontational!

You are a reporter

Purpose: Practise framing questions that will elicit in-depth information.

Pupils prepare questions to interview a peer. This could be related to things they have been doing at school or home. They can use the questions to survey others and report back on their findings.

Question awards

Purpose: Celebrate and encourage effective pupil questioning.

Pupils generate questions that might be nominated for 'question awards'. For example, the most creative, most thought-provoking or most controversial question (see page 57).

All views considered

Purpose: Challenge or contest a point of view that differs from your own appropriately and respectfully.

Pupils prepare posters with controversial statements. For example: 'There should be no chat rooms on the Internet', 'Man United is the best football team in the English Premiership', 'Capital punishment should be re-introduced for serious crimes' or 'You should not eat meat'.

   Place the generic questions cards (page 58) face up in the centre of the group. Display the posters and discuss why they are likely to produce a range of diverse opinions and what might have influenced people to develop the view they hold. Pupils suggest ways they can respond politely to a view with which they disagree. In the course of discussing one of the poster statements, group members must select a card to use in response to another pupil's views. Pupils' suggestions could be written on spare cards. Make time at the end to reflect on the value of the stems.

What questions would be useful to ask?

What are some possible explanations?

Do those two ideas agree?

How do you know?

Thinking on your feet: a time line

Purpose: Encourage pupils to generate questions to clarify their thinking.

Getting students to stand up can refocus them and activate their thinking. Therefore it makes sense to plan some questioning that requires pupils to be on their feet. A values continuum ranging from 'strongly agree' to 'strongly disagree', where pupils are asked to position themselves in relation to particular statements, is one way. Once positioned, question pupils about their stance, encouraging them to be flexible in their thinking and to change positions if convinced by the arguments of their peers. An alternative activity is to pin up a time frame, for example 1900 at one end of the classroom and 2000 at the other. Each pupil is given a card with an event printed on it, for example 'World War I' and 'Miners' Strike'. Pupils align themselves along the time frame continuum in chronological order of the events they have been given. This requires considerable questioning of each other to establish what they believe is the correct order.

Six thinking hats: questioning to review learning

Purpose: Encourage pupils to think critically, creatively and reflectively.

De Bono's six hat thinking is well known for encouraging different types of thinking. The next table (page 39) shows how teachers might use the strategy to ask questions that elicit creative, critical and reflective responses from pupils about their learning.

Using the six thinking hats framework to review learning

	General	English Literature focus	Maths Multiplication tables focus
White	What facts have you learnt? What information are you now sure about?	After reading the introduction, what can you say about the characters and setting?	What have you learnt in the last week?
Yellow	What are the highlights of your work?	What would you say are some of the positives of living in this era/place/family?	What multiplication tables do you now know well?
Black	What things could you have done better?	What difficulties do you anticipate for the characters in the future?	What multiplication tables do you need to work on?
Red	What do you feel about your accomplishments?	How have your feelings changed about the characters? What issues in the book concerned you?	How do you feel about your progress with learning tables?
Green	What could you have done differently?	If you were the author, how would you have started the story differently?	Is there another way you could learn your tables?
Blue	Overall, what would you say about your progress? What questions do you now have?	What issues has the author tackled and ignored? What questions would you like to ask the author?	Overall, what do you think about your understanding of multiplication?

SCAMPER

Purpose: Support the design of questions that encourage creative thinking.

Select the techniques that best suit your purposes, rather than use all seven at once. This strategy may be applied to the study of a text or a unit of work. It works well for many purposes, for example:

- Adapting a product
- Thinking about an issue differently
- Solving a problem more creatively
- Considering alternatives to existing structures, storylines, etc.

The following questions are designed around the book *The Wishing Cupboard* (Hathorn & Stanley 2002).

S	Substitute	Replace the items in the wishing cupboard drawer with the items you would include.
C	Combine	How might the story be different if Tran and Lan had opened the drawers of the wishing cupboard together?
A	Adapt	How would you adapt the design of the wishing cupboard to suit your purposes?
M	Modify Magnify	Retell the story from the perspective of the mouse that visited the wishing cupboard. What might Lan add to the wishing cupboard if some drawers were added?
P	Put to another use	What would the wishing cupboard be used for in your home?
E	Eliminate	If all the items were removed, what might the family members now want to include?
R	Reverse	What might have happened if Tran's grandmother had flown with her brother to find the special herb?

Three Cs and three Ps

Purpose: Provide a user-friendly questioning framework that combines the cognitive and affective domains.

This questioning model is a practical application of two of Bloom's domains: cognitive and affective. It requires pupils to critique, compare, make connections, consider a range of perspectives, personalise the issue/idea and prioritise.

	Think about it
Critique	What do you know and believe?
	What might you expect to happen?
	What factors need to be considered?
	What are the gaps or silences?
	Whose view dominates?
	What are the strengths and weaknesses?
Compare	What if you compare ...?
	What are the similarities between ...and ...?
	What are the differences between ...and ...?
Connect	If you put all the factors together, what are the big ideas?
	What connections can you make to what you already know?
	What relationships can you make?
	What are some of the causes and consequences?

	Feel it and act on it
Ponder perspectives	What is another way of thinking about this?
	What perspective is missing?
	How would the situation change if ...?
Personalise	If you had to choose ... what would you decide?
	What is your opinion?
	What do you care most about?
	Who might have a different point of view?
	How could you apply your learning to your life?

How does this fit with your thinking when we started the unit?

How does this relate to your situation?

Have you changed your ideas? If so, how and why?

How do your actions impact upon others?

Prioritise	What is the most important?
	What is the least important?
	Which point do you need to address first?
	What can you leave until later?

Frequently asked questions (and troubleshooting)

When do you tell pupils the answers?

In pupil-centred classrooms, pupils have the major responsibility for posing and finding out the answers to their own questions. If teachers answer their questions, pupils will not have anything to answer themselves. However, there are situations when teachers should answer pupil questions to avoid pupil frustration and to allow them to move forward. Some examples include when:

- the necessary resources are unavailable or unsuitable
- pupils have tried to answer their questions for a reasonable amount of time
- an answer is needed for pupils to complete the task
- pupils are becoming frustrated or discouraged by dead ends to their answer seeking
- a simple answer will allow pupils to proceed onto a more complex task.

Can teachers ask too many questions?

Yes. Generally teachers ask a lot of questions – mostly procedural or disciplinary – but don't provide enough time for pupils to ask questions of interest to them. As previously discussed, questioning can easily assume a quiz show style if some planning has not been considered. When teachers ask too many questions, pupils often feel uncomfortable and inhibited. Aim for quality not quantity. A comment or statement followed by wait time can be occasionally used as an alternative to a question.

How do you assess questions?

The type of questions that pupils ask, such as critical, creative or reflective questions, are generally assessed informally. For example, through observation of pupil participation in whole class and small group discussions, and through questions pupils pose for project work, inquiry units and in reflective journal entries. A rubric has been developed for this book (see pages 59–60); however, rubrics work most effectively when they are jointly constructed by the teacher and pupils and have gradations of quality to meet the individual needs of the class.

Audio or videotaping a discussion is particularly useful for assessment of teacher and pupil questioning.

How do I build questions into my plan?

While questions are asked spontaneously in relation to pupil comments and lesson outcomes, planning of some key questions or discussion statements can improve the quality of questioning. If an inquiry-based unit is being undertaken, some focus questions can be generated at different stages of the inquiry process. Similarly, planning of specific questions can occur for different stages of a lesson. Questions should be written as closely as possible to what would be said in class, such that the written planning is a form of rehearsal. When questions are carefully planned, there is less likelihood of rephrasing and refining the question, which can cause confusion about what the teacher is really asking; and the possibility of asking more than one question at a time is increased.

Some points to remember when planning key questions are:

- Make questions clear and succinct
- Sequence questions in a logical order
- Match questions to pupils' experience and abilities
- Focus on eliciting higher-order thinking, generalising and conceptualising rather than recalling factual information.

Generic questions for stages of a unit/lesson

Beginning

- What do you need to do/know to get the task done?
- What different methods/approaches could be useful?
- How does this task connect with other tasks you have done?
- How will you ensure everybody contributes to the task?

During

- What do you remember from last time that may be helpful?
- How are you progressing?
- Do you need to change your strategies?
- What information do you still need?

End

- What achievements are you most proud of?
- What is something that has taken your interest?
- What is something new that you have learnt?
- What is something that still confuses or puzzles you?

How can I improve my questioning?

Planning questions and reflecting on questions is a good start. Video and tape recording a discussion is an excellent strategy for review purposes. It is common for teachers to be surprised at the number and type of questions they ask. Use the checklist of *Traps to avoid* (page 50) as an audit tool and draw up an action plan that targets areas for improvement. Another strategy is to ask a colleague to act as a critical friend and give specific feedback on your questioning strategies. Through introducing different questions types and questioning strategies, you will have the opportunity to move across and between theory and practice, increasing your general understanding of the questioning processes in the teaching and learning contexts.

What if pupils don't ask good questions?

Ask any parent and they will tell you that children ask endless and complex questions. However, they may be reluctant to do so at school. The following ideas might assist to encourage pupil questioning:

- Model interesting and varied questions.
- Make time for questions throughout the lessons.
- Instead of asking pupils questions, tell them the answers and have them pose appropriate questions.
- Display questions around the room with the answers that have been found by pupils.

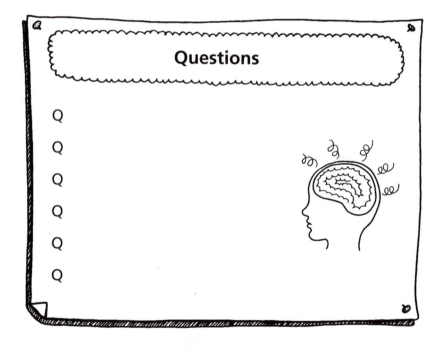

- Create situations that arouse pupil curiosity.
- Initiate awards for the best questions. Categories could be determined by the class (see page 57).

Question Award

Awarded to ___Edward___

For the most ___creative question___

Question ___Why do popcorns turn into different shapes?___

Signed ___Suellen Major___

- Use pupil questions for discussions.
- Ask questions that pupils want/need to seek outside of the classroom.
- Discuss different types of questions and identify them when used.
- Have pupils design quizzes for others.
- Use questioning taxonomies and strategies to structure and vary questions.
- Play games with questions. For example, make a die with question starters on each face or play a lucky dip question game. (See the Q-matrix activity, page 29.)

Tips for the teacher

Tips for more effective questioning

DO

- Set up a classroom where questioning is encouraged.
- Give appropriate feedback for the types of questions you want to encourage. For example: What a creative question.
- Pose questions to suit the purpose. What do you really want to find out about?
- Plan questions before the lesson.
- Ask different types of questions.
- Use questions to challenge, extend thinking and raise curiosity.
- Make time for pupil questions.
- Display questions around the room that capture pupils' imagination and may challenge them to find the answers.
- Jointly construct lists of great questions that have always puzzled pupils about things, people, places, events, etc. Encourage them to seek out the answers.
- Model self-talk and self-questioning.
- Ask unconventional questions.
- Ensure that pupils understand the question.
- Allow time for pupils to think of an answer.
- Generally ask less complex questions first.
- Think carefully about your responses to answers and pupil questions.

- Use pupil responses to ask further questions.
- Be interested in pupil questions but, if you want pupils to find out the answers to their own question, avoid answering them.
- Reflect on your techniques and strategies. Consider videotaping a class discussion or eliciting feedback from peers or pupils.

Traps to avoid

DON'T

- Ask a string of questions simultaneously.
- Ask ambiguous questions.
- Neglect to sustain the question with probes.
- Ask a question and answer it too (rhetorical question).
- Target the same pupils every time or ask only pupils you think will give the best responses.
- Use questioning as a behavioural management tool, for example, to discipline pupils for not listening.
- Begin with a very challenging question before pupils are feeling confident.
- Ask predictable questions, always the same type and order.
- Consistently use quiz-style questioning.
- Allow inadequate think time for higher-order questions.
- Fail to respond positively and constructively to an answer.
- Overlook the implications of answers.
- Fail to build on responses.
- Insist on giving verbal feedback to every answer.

Assessment and record keeping

Some formal record keeping is useful for assessing the development of pupils' questioning strategies and skills, and for evaluating the effectiveness of the teaching focus on questioning. While ongoing monitoring may occur informally, evidence is needed to demonstrate pupil improvement, albeit in a qualitative way, to parents when reporting and for school record-keeping purposes.

Post-it notes may be helpful for anecdotal observations about the type of questions pupils initiate and their responsiveness to questions in small group and whole class discussions. Notes can then be transferred to formal record-keeping procedures. A proforma approach to record keeping is provided on pages 61–4, and the rubric (pages 59–60) is an alternative way in which pupils can self-assess their achievements.

Example of partially completed *Self-Assessment Rubric* (see pages 59–60)

Name: _John_

Circle the description that applies to you.

Question-asking	**I always** ask questions confidently; to clarify my thinking; to seek more information; to critically analyse information; and to get feedback from others.	**I usually** ask questions confidently; to clarify my thinking; to seek more information; to critically analyse information; and to get feedback from others.	**I sometimes** ask questions confidently; to clarify my thinking; to seek more information; to critically analyse information; and to get feedback from others.	**I never** ask questions confidently; to clarify my thinking; to seek more information; to critically analyse information; or to get feedback from others.
Question-answering	**I always** use think-time when responding to complex questions; respect different ideas; and am flexible in my thinking.	**I usually** use think-time when responding to complex questions; respect different ideas; and am flexible in my thinking.	**I sometimes** use think-time when responding to complex questions; respect different ideas; and am flexible in my thinking.	**I never** use think-time when responding to complex questions; respect different ideas; or am flexible in my thinking.
Question types	**I always** consider the purpose for my question; and use different types of questions for different purposes.	**I usually** consider the purpose for my question; and use different types of questions for different purposes.	**I sometimes** consider the purpose for my question; and use different types of questions for different purposes.	**I never** consider the purpose for my question; or use different types of questions for different purposes.

Proformas for the classroom

Independent Investigation Guiding Questions

 ## Key questions to get started

What do I already know?

What are my key questions?

How will I plan to answer my questions?

What are my personal learning goals?

 ## Key questions to keep going

What could I do better?

What do I need to do to achieve my goals?

 ## Key questions for further learning

How have my ideas changed?

How well do I think I went?

What new learning goals can I set?

Reflection Question Strips

What team skills did your group use?

What did you like about the activity?

What could have been done to make the activity more useful?

What did you contribute to the group?

What aspects of your work need to be improved?

What skills have you improved?

What goals do you have now?

What would you do differently next time?

How have your ideas changed over this unit?

What did you learn?

What learning strategy worked best for you?

How well did you meet your learning goals?

Metacognition Strips: Getting Thinking Started

What do you already know about this topic?

What do you want to find out?

What questions do you have?

How will you source the information?

Why might we be studying this topic?

How might you start this task?

What do you need to think about to get the task completed?

What are your big questions?

How has your thinking changed?

What sort of thinking would be useful for this task?

What goals do you need to set for your learning?

Question Awards

Question Award

Awarded to _____

For the most _____

Question _____

Signed _____

Question Award

Awarded to _____

For the most _____

Question _____

Signed _____

Question Award

Awarded to _____

For the most _____

Question _____

Signed _____

Golding's Generic Questions

Why did you say that?

Is that a good enough reason?

Is that what you meant?

What are some possible explanations?

When would that not happen?

How do you know?

What would the consequences be?

Do those two ideas agree?

How is that different from what was said?

What questions would be useful to ask?

What have we found out?

Self-assessment Rubric

Name: _____

Circle the description that applies to you.

	I always	I usually	I sometimes	I never
Question-asking	ask questions confidently; to clarify my thinking; to seek more information; to critically analyse information; and to get feedback from others.	ask questions confidently; to clarify my thinking; to seek more information; to critically analyse information; and to get feedback from others.	ask questions confidently; to clarify my thinking; to seek more information; to critically analyse information; and to get feedback from others.	ask questions confidently; to clarify my thinking; to seek more information; to critically analyse information; or to get feedback from others.
Question-answering	use think-time when responding to complex questions; respect different ideas; and am flexible in my thinking.	use think-time when responding to complex questions; respect different ideas; and am flexible in my thinking.	use think-time when responding to complex questions; respect different ideas; and am flexible in my thinking.	use think-time when responding to complex questions; respect different ideas; or am flexible in my thinking.
Question types	consider the purpose for my question; and use different types of questions for different purposes.	consider the purpose for my question; and use different types of questions for different purposes.	consider the purpose for my question; and use different types of questions for different purposes.	consider the purpose for my question; or use different types of questions for different purposes.

© S. Godinho and J. Wilson, *Helping your pupils to ask questions*, Routledge, 2008.

Planning	I always use questions to assist in the planning, organising and reviewing of my work.	I usually use questions to assist in the planning, organising and reviewing of my work.	I sometimes use questions to assist in the planning, organising and reviewing of my work.	I never use questions to assist in the planning, organising or reviewing of my work.
Self-monitoring	I always ask questions to check my progress; assess my learning; make connections between ideas; and set future goals.	I usually ask questions to check my progress; assess my learning; make connections between ideas; and set future goals.	I sometimes ask questions to check my progress; assess my learning; make connections between ideas; and set future goals.	I never ask questions to check my progress; assess my learning; make connections between ideas; or set future goals.
Risk-taking	I always am prepared to ask questions about tentative ideas; ask creative questions; and challenge ideas different to mine.	I usually am prepared to ask questions about tentative ideas; ask creative questions; and challenge ideas different to mine.	I sometimes am prepared to ask questions about tentative ideas; ask creative questions; and challenge ideas different to mine.	I never am prepared to ask questions about tentative ideas; ask creative questions; or challenge ideas different to mine.

An effective question I recently asked: _____
_____
_____

Two aspects of questioning I want to improve: _____
_____
_____

My plan of action is: _____
_____
_____

Assessment Checklist

Name: _____

	Often	Some-times	Never	Comments
Question-asking				
Asks questions confidently				
Initiates questions in a discussion context				
Asks clarification questions				
Asks divergent questions				
Asks questions to extend understanding				

	Often	Some-times	Never	Comments
Directs questions to peers				
Asks questions to get feedback from others				
Takes risks with question asking				
Asks critically analytical questions				

Question-answering

	Often	Some-times	Never	Comments
Allows wait time before answering complex questions				
Is prepared to explore tentative ideas				

	Often	Some-times	Never	Comments
Contests ideas and opinions appropriately				
Respects that people have different perspectives and points of view				

Planning

	Often	Some-times	Never	Comments
Uses effective questions to focus an investigation				
Uses questions to organise an approach to a task				
Uses questions to review work				

	Often	Some-times	Never	Comments
Self-monitoring				
Uses questions to self-regulate and monitor progress				
Uses questions to make connections between ideas				
Uses reflective questions to assess learning				

Further reading

Abbott, C. and Godinho, S. (2001) *Thinking Voices: Developing Oral Communication Skills*, Curriculum Corporation, Carlton.

Barnes, D. (1975) *From Curriculum to Communication*, Penguin Books, Middlesex.

Brown, G. and Wragg, E. (1993) *Questioning*, Routledge, London.

Cam, P. (1995) *Thinking Together: Philosophical Inquiry for the Classroom*, PETA, NSW.

Cazden, C. (1988) *Classroom Discourse*, Heinemann, Portsmouth, NH.

Clements, S. and Godinho, S. (2003) *Read and Reflect*, Curriculum Corporation, Carlton.

Chambers, A. (1994) *Tell Me: Children, Reading and Talk*, PETA, NSW.

Costa, A. (1991) *The School as a Home for the Mind*, Hawker Brownlow, Vic.

Dalton, J. (1995) *Adventures in Thinking*, Nelson, South Melbourne.

de Bono, E. (1994) *CoRT Thinking Teacher's Notes*, Hawker Brownlow, Vic.

Dillon, J. (1988) *Questioning and Teaching: A Manual of Practice*, Croom Helm, London.

Erbele, R.F. (1972) 'Developing education through SCAMPER', *Journal of Creative Behaviour*, vol 6, pp 192–203.

Gross, M. *et al.* (2001) *Gifted Students in Primary Schools: Differentiating the Curriculum*, A Gerric Publication, The University of NSW, Sydney.

Golding, C. (2002) *Connecting Concepts: Thinking Activities for Students*, ACER Press, Melbourne.

Hathorn, L. and Stanley, E. (2002) *The Wishing Cupboard*, Lothian Books, South Melbourne.

Jensen, E. (1998) *Super Teaching, Focus Education*, Flagstaff Hill, South Australia.

Kiddey, P. and Waring, F. (2001) *Success for All*, Curriculum Corporation, Carlton.

Krathwohl, D., Bloom, B. and Masior, B. (1964) *Taxonomy of Educational Objectives: The Classification of Educational Goals: Handbook 2.* Affective Domain, McKay, New York.

McKenzie, J. (2000) *Beyond Technology*, FNO Press, Washington.

Ministry of Education (1989) *Learning to Learn: Investigating Effective Learning Strategies*, Melbourne.

Lipman, M. (1988) *Philosophy Goes to School*, Temple University Press, Philadelphia.

Murdoch, K. and Wilson, J. (2004) *Learning Links*, Curriculum Corporation, Carlton.

O'Brien, K. and White, D. (2001) *The Thinking Platform*, KD Publications, Marayong, NSW.

Pohl, M. (2000) *Learning to Think, Thinking to Learn*, Hawker Brownlow, Melbourne.

Pohl, M. (1997) *Teaching Thinking Skills in the Primary Years*, Hawker Brownlow, Melbourne.

Wilks, S. (1995) *Critical and Creative Thinking*, Heinemann, Portsmouth, NH.

Wiederhold, C. with Kagan, S. (1995) *Cooperative Learning and Higher-Level Thinking: The Q-Matrix*, Kagan Cooperative learning, San Juan Capistrano, California.

Wilson, J. and Wing Jan, L. (1993) *Thinking for Themselves: Developing Strategies for Reflective Learning*, Eleanor Curtain Publishing, South Yarra.

Wragg, E.C. and Brown, G. (2001) *Questioning in the Primary School*, Routlege Falmer, London.

Wragg, E.C. and Brown, G. (2001) *Questioning in the Secondary School*, Routlege Falmer, London.